GW00497342

Gallery Books
Editor Peter Fallon
THE MOUTH OF A RIVER

Seán Lysaght

THE MOUTH OF A RIVER

Gallery Books

The Mouth of a River
is first published
simultaneously in paperback
and in a clothbound edition
on 15 May 2007.

The Gallery Press
Loughcrew
Oldcastle
County Meath
Ireland

www.gallerypress.com

ISBN 978 1 85235 419 0 *paperback*
     978 1 85235 420 6 *clothbound*

A CIP catalogue record for this book
is available from the British Library.

Contents

for Chris and Lynda Huxley

PART ONE

Tarsaghaunmore

Elements

A first robe of words: a shoal of flies
above the fresh yellow of the furze,
insistence of earth and air, when Cromwell's god
and his ladies never passed this way,

just some dried orange peel
to mark a hiker's *déjeuner*. This might not
be enough — but it's all too much for a heron
that lifts its shriek into the distance, and deserts.

Then only sky remains in a window-hole,
stone's absence at the edge of stone
as seen by labouring men before a frame
was fitted to save a dream of stars.

The New Rucksack

Wouldn't you think he'd relax at home
and not be bothering us with his excitement,
said the stones.

I can keep an eye on the pool
above the footbridge,
said the big block of quartz.

I can keep a secret,
said the rowan.
The grey crow comes to me in the evening.

As my word is my bond,
said the stonechat,
we'll be up there in the myrtle gossiping away.

I can see him from up here.
He's on his way again,
said the lark.

Wait till you see the new rucksack!
said willy wag in the car park.
He shouldered it like a priest
getting ready for Mass.

Lazy Beds

You come to deny the day I held you
as you cried with hunger.

Those Yankees you worked for
couldn't have coped with such grief,

not like me who has a use
for your ghost on its pallet of oat straw.

Even the wind
through the empty window

can't blow without these words.
And it's your starved ribs I need

to figure out those ridges
as you lie there in your longing,

as you arch in the spasm of love
when the eldest son enters.

Merlin at Tarsaghaunmore

This is where the wizard lives,
still being realized
to cleave a range over the heatherings of a morning,
a surprise out of the mist.
This is where the horizon keeps an old nimble jack
away from the chattering city,
so no one can repute him to a bad end,
and no industry can exile him any farther.

He needs nothing more than the posts
he nominates with his feet,
this wire, this river bank,
this facing of stones to accommodate his desert eye,
and these two foxholes on the far side,
the stops of a flute he plays
when he lifts the glittering river.

But could you find him if you looked?
There has to be another god to upstage,
a different day that starts with maps,
and just as you stop for a eucharist of sandwiches
suddenly Pipit, the redeemer, is gone —
and there he is, with the mountain on his shoulders!
He's carrying the valley's only song!

Casadh na Leice

Bend at the rock wall.
The widening eye of the moor,

its lid lifted
by the tail of a salmon.

Brave water horse of heroes
attempting to storm the poachers' town.

Death-lane that opens after rain
(the only way in)

and shuts again in dry weather —
cutting off the escape.

Waiting room of dark water
with the eggs of the ice age,

the bright body cloaked
in clouds and turf smoke.

A furious modesty
kicks in the rape of the net.

A stone axe to hand
finally strikes, and denies it.

Grilse

Amazing what a fly
on a limp tail can do
to the strongest, the bravest:

lever it out of the weight of night,
beach its brightness at the darkest pool.

Oh, this is not the white of light,
these are the scales of stars.

Cover it, quick,
and get this bag out of here.

A Midge Charm

Breeze god
> get up and scatter the armies of the itchy witch

Rain god
> ruin their gathering veil

Cloud god
> forbid this travesty of your image

Horse god
> shake your heathery mane

Water god
> splash your frown of ripples

Hill god
> lead us out of all hollows

Turf god
> preserve us with your smoke

Frost god
> put on your white coat
> and lock them all away!

Sandpiper

This sentry patrols
the river's trench,
lamenting his moorland station.
Watch that fishing rod!

Under a cliff of peat,
hunched wings sweep
down the throat of a pool
on their own reflection.

He shadows the finnock
in their day of fear,
then reappears complaining
in a house of foxgloves.

The lonely bird salutes
because instinct has ordered,
performs his needy bow
for an absent-minded angler —

so little here to show
for a winter! No bright
colours out of Africa,
no badge of a tropical campaign,

only a pair of handy wings
to measure destiny:
Tarsaghaunmore to Guinea Bissau,
Srahnamanragh to Dakar,

from a sultry drumming shore
to guard the eggs
on a windy gravel flush
beside a clump of rushes.

Montbretia

When montbretia
finally looked out of its flower in late July

it saw a garden of deep water at its doorstep —
hardly the lawn it expected!

Everything shivered when dragonfly
stopped in its hover to say hello.

Salmon days in the redds!
Otters at the window weaving water!

But could this flower love itself
throughout the grey?

Would it not be swayed
by its diminished image

on the mirror of sky mountain?
How would it cope with the idiot sheep

bleating their woes all day
to the silent cliffs?

Poor montbretia,
nodding alone at the pool,

regretting its roots as I pass.

A Discovery

August, an evening, and I'd had enough
of the meandering river's question.
That web of fields and abandoned walls
in the valley's upper reaches were in my fatigue
with the stone's character of toil and heartbreak
as the lidded evening thickened and I took
the peat of the river bank in my booted stride.
I walked *andante*, to the metronome of an ending,
when another crossed the twilit footbridge
con brio, in his day's closing passage,
making for a grassy patch near the river
and unloading a bulky pack of gear.
Who was this loner setting up for the night?
He had, of course, reached his wilderness
just as I was passing under cover
of the river's noise on the rising turf-bank opposite.
I supposed he wasn't there to be hailed
or challenged by someone who had got there
earlier, who would spoil an original story,
and I kept going, so as not to be seen.
And yet, here are the prints in that peat,
that steady exhalation where a range is stored
of a river diminishing to the cold
of spawning water at the top of its catchment.
The camper could have looked up from his preparations
to read the figure disappearing downstream
who had, in his turn, established his own pitch
where he imagined no one had been watching.
I held my pace steady in my aloneness
and never looked back until now, to revise
that favourite valley into a stage for eyes
and to realize how happily I walked
into the script of my own occasion.

The Drover's Stick

in memory of Paddy McHugh

Following on from your stories —
how you drove your cattle

through the night-roads to the fair —
you brought out your stick collection

and gifted me what I asked for,
the one I have to keep,

a hazel newly cut from the roadside
in Nephin's shadow.

Its white eyes peep
where someone planed the stems.

If I never make your miles
along your moorland river

this drover's stick
will remember another pace

as it seasons in the corner
within the busy house.

I take its weight again
and test its swing in the air,

like the wand you waved at dawn
when you conjured your given way

and drove those thirsting shoulders on
towards the lightening horizons.

PART TWO

The O———

I leave Dublin to-morrow for M—— house. It is situated in the county of ———, on the north-west coast of Connaught, which I am told is the classic ground of Ireland.

Lady Morgan, *The Wild Irish Girl*

I

Cruikshank's assistant was working late
on the second volume. This was the hardest plate,
'The Mouth of the River O———' in deepening twilight
from the darkest sketch in all of Bartlett.
Five guttering candles couldn't redeem
his back-lane studio from its winter gloom.
His scratching pin was drawn across the copper
like an angler's fly one imperial sunset later
on the same metallic sheen, in fading colours
as the first bats fluttered over the river.
He struggled in the current of a spendthrift life,
keeping his debts a secret from his scolding wife,
like any man paying the price for a passion,
figuring the boat and the pile of net astern
in the darkest strokes, then alders and sycamores
over a rocky gorge, and shadowy waters
where the sky's shimmer was lost to an overhang
on the far side — what terrible conditions
to have to work in! These were the limitations
of the genre, omitting the mink's yelp and the owl's
call, and the torture of midges as the scene was swallowed
by darkness. But the scratching hook persisted
in the hunt for silver. He had creditors insisting
on being paid and a month's rent was overdue,
then his wife's glaring reproach,
                                    'Where were you?'

II

Among the O———'s beginnings there's this stream
that leaks from a gully on a remote mountainside.
A hag overlooks the place, with its top of heather
silver-stemmed with age, and a peaty bank
like an old cow releasing the first water.
There's a single oak there too,
surviving in the shelter of a cutting carved by the stream,
and an old crow's nest built from fallen
fingers of the tree. The trail sags like a hammock
into this crossing, where water pours over
stones, and you lose all birdsong under
the noise of running water, only the raven
honks to say thanks for the leftovers.

A reminder, then, where a man bends down
to kiss the stream, that he meets an image
of his own thirst, framed in the shadowing sky.

III

The O—— was every river he'd lived by:
Owenmore, Owenglas, Owenwee,
Owenduff, Oweninny, Owengarve,
formed when a great bird stood in that valley
and left the emphatic print of its claws.
The spate had a channel from the high heather
to the estuary and its runway of water
where running salmon crowded like memories.

Between those two the river fought
the outline of its fated course.
                                    It meandered
over its basin and made silted pastures
in the loops where hunger and folklore could survive.
The till of glaciers was sifted along its banks,
pine roots collapsed, the turf, in section,
dried and, still not content, the O——
abandoned one channel, to force its way
along another bed of land where fish could run.

After a dry Spring, when honeysuckle
raised its shoots in despair, you'd wonder
where the next flood would come from.

It was hard to think that these stale pools
could host the urgent passage of warriors from the sea.

IV

It was the same sea reshuffling the shore
at the windward edge of the sandy cemetery,
and the same ground where his bones used to rest
until one January storm finally made a break in the wall,
and the Council knew that history had a formidable enemy.
On winter tides a seal would appear
out of the surf to check the progress of skulls
and other bones falling from the bank, until the head
itself was threatened that had sung it all one time.
And then it happened, that dull, unavoidable
commotion of the damned ocean pounding at the base
of those small grains of comfort he had come to love,
saying, 'This is the time now to release yourself
back to those waves where all life began.'
And the skull fell into the foam, and floated
where the flounder and bass ran in the shallows.
When another wave came, and it smashed,
it could have settled into the small mercy of sand.
But a fish had been alerted. And that was enough.

V

Then all the salmon knew, as they waited
in their archaic style somewhere in a bay.
Even in salt they could get traces of their native
gravel; they could smell the peat; they remembered
where algae came from, with mud
and stems of rushes. The water came flavoured
with sheep off those uplands; in the spate the fish sensed
cold stones washed by falling water,
and hands made numb by mountain rain.
Late in the year gusting winds shook
petals like confetti from the loosestrife
to announce that now was the time to begin the journey
back to the pools of home, as if someone had said,
'Isn't it time, son, you e-mailed your father?'
Conscience, or maybe a genome remembering
the river where they'd been born. Anyway,
against the drift of water, they began.

VI

The river ran the last stages of its journey
over stones that waves had heaped up
across its mouth, the wild sea being stronger.
This evening, as surfers packed up to go home,
a high tide was pushing foamy waves
closer to the lip of the bar, and in the commotion
of surf and brown waters of the river's spate,
sea trout were ready for migration.
They had braved it to the very top of the waves
where manes of water were being scattered
by a westerly breeze.
                    They knew from the taste of the bay
that this was the time to move.
                    When the next high wave
brought water over the bank of shingle
a few fish managed to riffle through.
Others, hesitating, saw tail-fins
disappear into the gloom of the surge
and they realized what instinct meant.
With their white flanks flashing at the surface
more and more of them rushed through into the O———
on each successive pulse of the racing sea,
until the tide turned and a moon was left
above the shimmer, wondering what had happened.

VII

Harry lay on the beach, reading again
as waves broke around the shrieking bathers.
The sand was kind, fallen from his shins.
Several boys tried to bury the body
of a friend, to have it re-emerge perfected
in the end, and run straight after its captors.
Harry was thinking of a high, exalted style
to take him on his journey or, even, whether
he wanted the effort of a story when the ice-cream van
churned a tune; why scan the ocean
for the boat that ends or starts a chapter
when you can join that snot-and-sand commotion:
'Two ninety-nines! And a packet of crisps!'
won at the van?
                    Such ice-cream cones
were nurtured like flames by barefoot athletes
in a pause in the games. Watched by Harry,
two visiting sisters walked to the waves
and did not notice the older man behind them,
attempting to live the life of a single mind.

VIII

The bay had an island for every day in the year.
The story was familiar, from springtime cold,
through the colours of summer, to the holly jolly
families on the beach at Christmas, but everyone
was too busy to watch each day
as it composed a year.
                          Only now and then
a butterfly paused on the grass to open the leaves
that said, 'Boys galloped in the shallows.'
This gave Harry an image for his instinctive theme.
He wanted the boats of myth in every inlet,
keels crunching gravel, heels at once
finding ground, and action, the plot holding
with the butterfly gone, no one selling cones,
the caravans closed up for the winter
so that, when a walker broached the coast
on a dreary day to count those painters' islands,
you'd see his own form in that light,
in March, or October, when local men
like hooded seals leaned on their sailboards
and went knifing among the reefs in wind;
they were in no mood to speak to anyone,
as the air in their own bay spirited them.

IX

As the old trades died, and currachs rotted
along the coast, it was needlework like Poppy's
that kept the craft alive. She was loyal
to her great-aunt Daisy who stitched the hours
of Britain's finest, but never cheered her Michael
home. It wasn't grief or defiance
that Poppy worked into those exotic leaves
as they spread their woollen stitch across her frame,
and there was no pathos meant where February
shook its veils of sleet across the bay
and the winds badgered her nerves.
                                        She lived
within that weather. No way would she be
rushed into buying curtains; passers-by
could invent titles for her solitude
like 'Woman at the Window' or 'Wife in Exile'.
She was so perfected in her living-room window
on those winter afternoons they let her loneliness be,
and she had time to make progress with her orange tree.

X

Every year he resolved to spend less
time on the river and get other things done,
but he couldn't resist the lure of moving fish.
In winter, time couldn't rest on his hands either,
when he discovered that his inventions
with hooks and bits of rubbish were capable
of catching, so he tied his own flies.
Greenwell's Glory, *Wickham's Fancy*, *Butcher* —
all these traditional names
gave way to Harry's new creations.
He made these from odds and ends
filched from Poppy's sewing-box.
                                        'Where's my red?'
she said one day as she searched for wool
to finish the strawberry in the border —
'Harry, have you taken my stuff again
for those flies of yours, have you?'
So she chided him in good humour.

'You'd better catch some trout next time!'

The red fly was christened *Poppy's Fancy*
and it proved successful that year
in Spring for brown trout.

XI

Johnny still held out where the poles
could go no farther; the track came
to an end at his cottage in the mountains.
He had two dogs to guard a territory
of rhododendron — his 'rosy dandrums' —
and five or six acres of derelict fields.

The district nurse arrived once a week
to ask him if he was all right, which he was.
He said, 'I'm fine out. Fine out,'
although he was usually in when she called.
(In summer she scarcely crossed his threshold.)

The dogs sniffed the bright globe of her car.
One of them squirted at a hubcap
before it left, swayed by the potholes
of the untarred track, allowing peace
to return to Johnny's valley where he lived
by choice.
            He would end his days with his native
weather, predicting rain by the shades of distance
in the hills, among the other shades, his people.

XII

Who said that nothing ever happened there?
Johnny had time to study the hills and their depths of grey.
He was sure the day would be fine when Slievemore
stood out like a canvas by Paul Henry.

When he picked up a walking stick —
today he chose white ash — the dogs knew
they were setting out to check the cattle
and see if those horses left by the tinkers
were still about the place.
                              His path followed
the winding course of the river, along its peat-banks,
across the gravel flushes the floods
of winter left; it crossed the pasture that still
greened every summer between the river's
loops.
        His collies' yin and yang bolted
ahead of him; they rose a snipe from a drain
and eventually found the four horses idling
at the base of a heathery slope. The dogs turned
them onto a ridge above the river. Then Johnny
called them back in his deep neglected idiom,
'Come home ou'a that!' His words commanded
their magpie colours and their wild life
returning down, as the horses stood like legends
over them.
            In this way the sun had memories
to set on.
            Johnny picked his way home in the glare,
among the flaring blooms of *feileastrams*.

XIII

This was not one of those days when salmon
ran in churning water but, if they didn't
and the water of knowledge was clear, Harry could think
of other things to ask Johnny besides fish.
At his questions about rights and river banks
Johnny wandered in his old man's childish manner,
the way that age migrates back to its source.

He described several men, with dogs,
covering every slope and ridgeback
for sheep. The mountains were busy again.
They called the collies on and on
till the whole land sounded with their voices.
Grouse took off from the shoulder of the summit
to take their indignation down to the shore of a lough
where a giant was buried. It was deep enough.
Then, on a stony whaleback, clear of sheep,
a few bored lads started throwing rocks,
not knowing what their carelessness was causing
three hundred metres down, to other men.

'Is it long since you were up there yourself?'
Harry asked.
            'About three years.'
                        The answer
faded off the cliffs without an echo.
It stayed with the eagles and all the voiceless dead.

XIV

He wanted her deep, with the whisker of his hackle
on her glides. He wanted to stand against her
as she gushed out in streams from his steady thighs.
He would follow her from the windy *feileastrams*
to catch her first laughter at the foam of the weir,
and be there to hear it echoing from the last flood.
There was always too much breeze for her silks to steady
to a mirror where he could see himself
but, still, a promise blew from the higher pools,
to wrestle with her, when the *cleamhadh deorán* left.

Before that could be she meandered maddeningly
through shallow streams that were someone else's
nursery at some other time, not now.
And he wondered, as he sweated in the heavy air,
if he would ever find the woman the flood applauded.
Nothing in the signature of the pond skaters
told him anything about where she'd be.
As he toiled on across the gravel banks
he heard the stones kiss under his boots.

XV

'Did you catch anything?' Poppy asked
cheerfully when Harry walked in.
                                    'No,
too bright, and the river's too low.'
He stood in the kitchen with the white husks
of his new waders padding out his shins.
'I don't know how,' she scolded, as he watched
the filling pool of the kettle. He was cold and hungry
from another blank day on the O———.
Every trip up there spaced him out,
*thrown back upon yourself, and forward
against the mystery and majesty of nature.*

Such talk was all very well
if you weren't exercised by the hunter's need.
But Harry had hammered the blade of the river's glare
all day, and every fish withheld its legend.

XVI

The river was rain,
                    then rain for a second day.
All weather lore went limp, like a damp page.
The sky was level with his frown.
                              The air bounced.
The dripping heather and every shining stone
for fourteen miles were flowing towards the sea
through the passage of a famous spate stream.
All over the catchment the day said flood.
Tons of water hammered past the house.
A brown monster writhed across the fields,
raging to be over, to settle back to the sea,
to be again the scullery maid of the bog,
the whole summer washing the glacier's stones.

The foam came down in fluffy stacks,
white and stiff like catering hats.
Sand martins flew past their sunken homes,
but the sheep under the whin weren't interested
in flowers wasted, buttercups gone under.
Long brambles snagged with baler twine
trailed dead grass across her countenance!

And then, abroad in the grey dawn, alone
on the moor, an angler moved through all of this,
carrying a silver salmon hanging from his fist
in fulfilment of its own weight of light.

XVII

When the hills had clouded with another bout
of grief, when heather shoots, red rowan
and matted fleece had all been disburdened,
the spate stream toiled in its narrow bed
past browsing cattle.
                Harry was stung
by her words and his own meagre catch,
but he wouldn't give up, he had to pay
the tribute of those streams, as if, by some
stroke of fortune as a boy, he had killed
and tasted a creature reserved for a god.
So he drove away as soon as the rain abated
and, half an hour later, had tackled up.

Thigh-deep in those leaves, in that rank vegetation
crowding to the river's edge, he walked
the abandoned swords of yellow flag
to the place above the bridge he knew
held virgin grilse.
                They floated
in their otherworld above a sunken stone,
riding the current, as something held them taut
towards the redds where they'd been spawned.

XVIII

It had to be right this time. He was sure.
He tried to concentrate on the bolt of the road
unfurling under his tyres, counting the markings —
but no, if there was such a thing as a salmon
anywhere, there had to be salmon on the O—— today.

Zen said, 'Expect nothing.'
                  He'd try.
Into the long track to Johnny's place.
Park smartly. Get the waders out —
all this bloody gear! Change from the shoes.
Then the rod, connect the two sections,
put the line through the rings, like a —
no time for that now; forget scenery.
Two flies, a shrimpy one at the end,
with a bumble on the dropper (*Kingsmill Moore*).
Test the knots. Get the bag and net.
Car keys. Lock.
               Away at last.
The thump of his waders on the road, across the shingle,
a first cast into the throat of the stream,
worth a try here, but not for long.
Poll a' Chonnie.
              Pollín Dubh.

XIX

Poll a' Chonnie. Pollín Dubh.
The two best holding pools. A trek.
Lovely water.
                    A splashing avenue.
                                        The wind.
The stream gathered tight like a bundled curtain
rushing against the bank, a deep muscle
toiling under the willows before it spreads
to where he'll be in the tail of the pool.
What it should be about. Flies drawn fast
at first, then fished lower in the darkness,
let fall into that small abyss
deep enough to drown a coach and four.
No sign of a fish, but all the time
a faith that a few still evade the poacher,
the seals, the drift nets, other anglers.
He forgets fatigue, and he takes little time
over his sandwich. There's another pool,
and a few stretches worth trying, and Zen
has said to expect nothing, which is just as well
because nothing is showing today, even
in this water, and last year they hit it right,
but that was August, and the flood was higher then.

XX

He kept going up the glen.
There wasn't much of the river left.
He'd soon be facing the steep flank of the mountain.
A ruined cottage was ahead of him
where someone had stooped to tend potatoes once
and called across the river to a dog that barked
within its territory, rehearsing an enemy.

The flow had reduced to a low trickle
over stones with a colouring of green slime.
This was where the fish would come in wintertime
to excavate their redds. Most of them
would also leave their lives with the pink cells
of their roe caught in the gravel. They fell back
in the current as ugly carcasses no one saw
going down.
            Then Harry passed the plot
the older folk had wrested from the bog.
After this there was only a quarter of a mile of *sheugh*
to the end of the catchment, and soon he would have to bow
to another withering failure —
                                until
the spur turned and a fine deep pool
was spread under the shelter of rowan trees.

XXI

There must have been a fault in the rock where the spate
had scoured out such a heavy reservoir.
Anything waiting within would sleep on a dream
of drift and pine-roots at the base of earth.
Day came into focus as a silted crag.
Now and then the head of a tinker's horse
ghosted on the surface.
                                    Then the labour of rain.

Harry stripped line from his protesting reel
and tested the air above the pool.
                                    He cast.
The fly tracked the dark water
like a satellite on its course among the frozen stars.
Lifted out at the end, it was flailed again,
taking a second purpose close to the first.
Harry watched it with his faith
that something had run so far upstream
when the flood was on.
                                    Suddenly, the fly locked.
A boil had spread where it had swum alone.
Harry lifted the rod and a salmon was on,
moving deep within the mountain's shadow.
He had no net, and no one to call to.
As Poppy was soon to finish her tapestry
the question was, could he finish with a fish?

XXII

For a long time the salmon refused to show. She ran
tense under the taut line where a fine V
revealed the position of the nylon.
Harry would steer her around the pool, keep her
clear of the snags on the far bank, but not haul —
he'd lost a good springer that way once.
He gave her time, and line when she needed it.

Then the reel screamed, and she breached, appealing
to the air that had given her the spate.

Her silver flank sank again.

She went patrolling the pool for the key to a puzzle
she had never known before —
                              such a small
buzz in her house, threatening everything!
To have made it all this way, to have survived
so many comrades taken in the mesh
of drift-nets, and then — betrayed at home!
What was it she hadn't sensed in that shrimp,
that little orbiting impostor?
They had taken zillions off Greenland
all winter. So why not snap at this,
for old times' sake? But to meet the ghost
of the mesh again, or a seal's hungry soul!

No, no, no, said her shaking head.
She clattered and thrashed,
                              clattered and thrashed,
as the heartless sheep continued to graze
and a raven flew over in its own life.

XXIII

The fish was tiring. She strained back to her element
but was summoned somewhere else.

                                      Harry had found,
at last, the life of so many stories, much of it
bullshit about salmon lies.
                    Lies.
                        Lies.
'You should've been here last night.' 'It'll be good
tomorrow.' 'It's still too high and too cold.'
His own truth was showing on the surface,
fixed to him, but it could break yet. Even with
careful knots the hook might come loose
at the final pull towards the landing place.

But the fish was tired. The circles were smaller.
He could steer now at will between the surges.
Then she lolled at the surface, on her side.
He started the haul through the shallows to a gravel
bank. He knew that taking a fish upstream
went against the rule book — but fuck the rules!
Just get 'em. That was the only fuckin' rule!

When the fish sensed the shallows she lunged once
more, but the brake on Harry's reel had broken
her heart, so it was easy to get her back
to this unrelenting dentistry. Then he grabbed the tail
and she landed.

XXIV

There she was, a three-pound grilse,
neutered now in his gravity, shouldered
into the grass. Caught. Harry grabbed
the neck, and levered out the fly.
The salmon made a choking noise
as if to say something that water understood
but could not be uttered in the element of air.
If fish squealed like rabbits Harry couldn't
kill them, but he was looking round for his priest,
or a stone, to knock her on the head and turn this life
into a dinner, as he had so many smaller trout,
when he hesitated.
                    Return that life. Show
the restraint you preach. Don't take her now and cancel
the passion you have known. Continue the story,
like those fine hen fish you put back
last year, restoring them to their life's chapters.
They were not any less yours for being saved.

Oh! It was time! It was time! She was losing breath!
Her pulse was fading!
                    The leaves of her gills were nearly
gone when he hoisted her body and rushed her
to the stream, standing astride her, until she shook
gently out of his hands to refuse him,
and then fade into the depth she came from.

XXV

The day had changed again.
                             It was dark overhead.
A breeze brought rain to the silent pool
and a frown to Harry's face. He left the spot
in a thickening downpour, threading his way
among the iris leaves and clumps of rushes.

Rain's empire again.
                       An occasional bleat
from the drenched flock, a distraction from the hiss
of the heavy drops getting in everywhere —

a pulse of the air, a choir half-remembered
by someone waking. He turned to look back
at a shaft of light sleeving a figure. There,
where he had restored the pool's oldest dreamer,
she held her place, like foxes crying in winter.
Not a face, but a voice grieving for his days
as he approached to listen:
                             'The noise was over,
the shock in my ears. I was standing. My hands.
So was he. Others on the ground. His tears.
Come away from this place. But where to?
Where could we go with his bleeding face?
He shook his head. No. No. Back
to a moment ago. Then voices. They realized.'

XXVI

The grief was high and cold, and it didn't know him.
Someone else's pain he had put back.
So he left it unattempted.
                    As he turned to go
the river was already rising. Small streams
higher up appeared as chalk lines
running down the mountain. Other waters
poured from the peaty sections, *pisse vache*,
or foamed in grassy drains. The water was clouding
and now it flooded across stones that had been dry.
A trickle found the collar of Harry's coat
and he shivered.
                    The cold was his only tribute.
He couldn't square his concerns with such pain.
He would not elevate his habits of indignation
to those. This was why he left her tower
of light, and returned to his proper twilight,
with a rod as his mark, setting him apart.

And still the water filled the O——— with its love.

XXVII

The spate stream was alive with fish.
                              At the steep
falls they appeared like the sea's commotion, exploding
from the flood. They seemed not to care if they twisted
on the plinth of a rock's obstacle and were beaten back
by the flow. Again and again with the buck of a muscle
they beat the surging stream and got through.
And smaller ones too, warrior sea trout
attended.
              Harry stayed on his side
of the river. He could not ford it now.

He noticed a van had appeared on the far bank.
Even in the gloom he knew it was the Heritage
Service — Fate, as he had been taught to translate,
and when his friend stepped out in her fetching style
his approach was easy.
                              'Nice day for a picnic!'

'I thought you might be here,' she shouted across
the charging water.
                              'I thought this place was a secret.
Even the man in the tackle shop hadn't heard of it.'

'You have to know the rivers in my job.
Welcome to the beforelife.'
                              'The what?'

XXVIII

'The beforelife!'
                    'I thought the name meant threshold.'

'Yes. A threshold, like a door to another world.
Look at those souls in the water on their journey.'

'But why the beforelife?'
                    'You mustn't have seen,'
she countered with that arrogant, stately head that came
of state service, and annual leave in the Himalayas.
'Look,' she nodded, as if they had been summoned.

The harvesters came from another century,
stooped in their madder skirts over the ground,
their faces cancelled by smears and weather,
back and buttock keeping line with the hills.
Then a shout to a child to clear the cattle out
because their hooves were wrecking the drills,
and over all the same burden of air,
as the shower eased to a clearing mist.

Downriver, men were building a fish-trap.
Another waded to the apex of the V
with a frame of mesh to set down in the stream.
'Aren't you going to stop them?' he challenged her.

'We don't do poachers,' she laughed. 'That's Fisheries.
And anyway, don't forget, this is the beforelife.'

XXIX

In those calm conditions the midges were a torment.
She noticed him rubbing his eyebrows, so she took a bottle
out of her pocket and slung it across the river.
'You need some of this stuff!' He sprayed his face
and neck, but there were still midges in his eyes as he threw
the bottle back to her and turned to look upstream.
Everywhere was earth and its implications: cropped fields,
kitchen plots and grazings. Flax-plants
and potatoes filled the tight enclosures with walls
and ditches between them and the stream
because the sandy soil by the river was the best.
'Everything's organic here!'
                    'Yes,' he replied,
'including the typhus. And so was the blight when it came.'
He marked how the figures conformed to the place
with their creaturely busy-ness. Many were spread
in the fields, while others just visible disappeared
towards the higher slopes.
                    'D'ya come here often?'
he mocked, as the woman scanned the ridges with binoculars.
Then the poachers passed, carrying the first
of their salmon, and he knew they were both invisible,
the way they didn't register in their eyes.
As his friend wrote data in her notebook he thought
that science couldn't redeem the pain stored there,
that the blind past was punishment enough.

XXX

Bhí taibhsí i mo bhéal, ach ní raibh mé
ábalta iad a shamhlú i dteanga mo mháthar.
B'in glór na ndaoine cromtha os cionn na ngort,
iad róghnóthach lena gcás a mhíniú.
Cúpla coiscéim eile agus bheinn leo,
ach d'fhan mé mar a raibh mé, i gceo
na míoltóga. Bhí na logainmneacha agam,
mar bhí Johnny ann mar mhúinteoir,
agus scéalta aige faoin bhfathach, 'Dháille Bhán,'
agus ainm na habhann miotasaí, 'An Tairseachán.'
Bhí a fhios agam go raibh sleáin ina luí,
agus málaí folamha ag feitheamh liom
le haghaidh prátaí a bhailiú,
ach bhíos róthógtha leis na bradáin
agus na bric gheala le dul anonn.
D'fhan mé mar a raibh mé, idir uaigneas
mo mhuintire fadó, agus an éacht
a bhí ar siúl san uisce, na héisc
chróga, agus an fios a bhaineann leo.
Bhí taibhsí i mo bhéal, ach ní raibh mé
ábalta iad a shamhlú i dteanga mo mháthar.

XXXI

'Did you get any?'
                    Harry turned round,
and there was Johnny again in his green wellingtons
and oilskin jacket. 'Yes,' he said. 'I got one,
but I put it back. I'm going away soon,
and I've no use for a salmon.' So he knows me now
as a dreamer and a traveller, Harry thought.
'They're killing too many anyway,' he added.

'Aye,' said Johnny, 'they are.' The old poacher
watched him from his eyes like clouded stone.
'Did you see any cattle?'
                          'No, only
those tinkers' horses.'
                        'Well, that heifer
is a walkin' curse. She'll be gone out to Maum.
And I've no dog to turn her.'
                             'The day's late,
Johnny. Can't it wait till tomorrow?'
                                      'It'll have to.'
'Come on, so. I'll have the tea with you.'

With that, they turned, the angler and the drover
on the *sraith* close to the stream. They moved
down among the stone ruins, past
the shaky footbridge, where the old man made dignified
complaint about its poor condition. 'You'd be better off
wading,' said Harry.
                     'You would not,' said Johnny.
'There's a great power of water there now.'

Then they climbed the track that took them away from the river.

XXXII

Another evening, inevitably,
because that's when our sun appears on the stage of the sea.
A bridge over a river. A weir. An estuary.
Harry has blanked again and chats to the bailiff.

The kelt of this song is spent, slipping back
over the brim of flooded stones.
Like the sea trout it heads back to the sea
as they dance on its glare with their promise.
So the butterfly can land to shut the wings of her book.

Have I given my vowels eyes
like timber the craftsman finishes well?
Have I crossed all the Os and followed their parallels,
the Áine in *fáinne* —

                    The bailiff breaks off.
He has to go after his cattle. They have broken
through rhododendron to the river and are fording it
to a grassy bank on the far side.
His figure diminishes as he turns them out,
back over the stony shallows, and home.
One of them shits in the water, for real.
Another, more nobly, pauses to drink and raises
its head, letting jewels fall back to this crown of a river.
Theories move on, but not the peace
that imagines a herder waving a stick at his beast
as both of them wade a filling tide at sunset.

Then a sudden comma, way down,
and a splash to say that the world can work
for a fish older than our pain;
                    and there she is again,
whom the Romans called *Salmo*, the leaper.

PART THREE

Bird Sweeney

Leavings

His name
a sibilance of aspens,
his mark there in mud,

hoof-prints of a stag
that galloped into absence
in this wood

and left a downy plume
adrift in mid-air,
leavings we follow

as we hunt ahead of death to hear,
beyond our bated breath,
his breath.

In the Wilderness

Sweeney whistled in the mouth of a river;
he was wigeon.

He dived in the surf of a lake;
he was smew.

His call came through from the stars,
as wind reared on the guyrope of midnight;
he was redwing.

He tickled the toes of the reeds in their beds;
he was dabchick.

He fenced on a catwalk of glittering water;
he was grebe.

He fell from the dome of day
to the floor of earth;
he was falcon.

Then he was phalarope, flitting in the hills of the grey sea.

Or shearwater, just clear of the waves in the wings of his life.

Eventually, he tilted homeward.

But the cleric had spotted him.

All of a sudden
he roared out 'Sweeney!'

And that spoiled everything.

The Wood at Dusk

The row with Ronan should have steeled him,
but it made him shy instead.

He avoided the obvious trees
when they went searching for him.

When they raised their poles with banners
into the leaves Sweeney skulked
in a grove of bracken, a woodcock
they would never find.

So they called it a day and left.
An hour later, at dusk,
he was roding over the canopy.

The Flight from the Tower

Since God had cursed him with wings
Sweeney believed he owed nothing
for this artifice.

He was a collapsed brolly
around the stem of his vigil,
a body riddled with quills.

He dreamed of other extensions
as pike-loads and oars
and clattery ladders.

When the day thinned in the ivy
he reached the great span of himself
for an armful of air

and the tower delivered him.
He twisted his cockpit
as he worked the rush of his feathers.

Magpies were out in the fields
inspecting the cages of sheep
they'd picked clean.

The bodies of sea birds were tossed,
in a tangle of seaweed,
beyond the sea's fiction.

Sweeney kept going.
He stayed clear
in the metre of his flying.

North Tawton

Sweeney flew on
to a yew tree
in North Tawton.

The church steeple was the shape of a witch's hat.
Everyone in the village
was dressed in black.

A hearse prowled across the square
with a seaman's coffin
draped in a Union Jack.

Then Sweeney surged into the blue
above them, a dove in mourning.

He jingled the keys of a robin's song
beside a gardener.

As a house sparrow
he arrowed into their eaves.

He mimicked the stars among their starlings.

When he flew back withershins
among the swallows they took no notice.

The blackbird answered his blackbird calls.

Even a tawny owl was taken in
by a note he commandeered from a woodpigeon.

But when he came to the crow
he couldn't find any black.
They had taken it all for the mariner's funeral.

The best he could manage was a grey mantle.

At once the crows saw through his disguise
and mobbed him over the hill.

The Cuckoo Option

Sweeney blundered into a glen
half-abandoned to alders.

A high-summer benediction
rose with the mist off a lake
bedded in a quilt of fields.

Twilight would be mothy and solemn —

Suddenly he heard shouting
in the trees:
           Fuck you!
Fuck you!
           For a moment, he thought,
'This will do.'

But when he saw the stripey top
and muscular physique he thought,
'Maybe it won't.'

Eagle

It was blowing a ferocious gale
when Sweeney slipped down
through a gap in the storm.
He vanished for days among the mountains.
Then he was trapped by a team of scientists.

'This hurts us more than it hurts you,' they said
as they tied a camera to his ankle
and strapped a tracker unit to his wing.
'We want to be with you in your wildness.
The camera will stay with you on your ledge;
it will keep sending back pictures,
even when your bone is as cold as stone.
We can track you as a dotted line.
We want to print copies of your life
so everyone in the office can say,
"This is mine! Now I know what to do with my Sundays!"'

But one of them didn't want it.
'No,' he said. 'Let me be the voice of the wild.
I'll give you the dark corries in my voice.
That bird wasn't made for loneliness.

It lives
as a wet
rock lives
in its own gleam,
as the broken
fern stays
in its angle,
as the wind
remains
in the warped
thorn. When
it cries

it will only
be answered
by another
who says,
"I have lived
in the cliff's
shadow
with my friends
from childhood,
Gale and Echo."'

Nonetheless, they logged
Sweeney's wanderings for three years.
Then the footage stopped.
They had to go after him.
The signal came from a remote glen.
They scanned it with binoculars
but there was no sign of Sweeney.
Six hours of searching later,
still no sign.
The signals said, right here,
but where was Sweeney?
The tall crags were keeping the secret
till someone shouted, 'Look!'
There was the camera on the scree,
and the little black box.

Sweeney had changed again.
He had stepped out of his shackles,

a wren.

The Hawk in the Orchard

A sparrowhawk flashed through the orchard
on the line of a previous sparrowhawk.
His centred eyes and instrument of feet
holding the thrush almost too far down
for the hooked bill to reach
told Sweeney how his kill would be.

The thrush was in the hawk's fate
as it flailed the evidence of shells
on a makeshift anvil. Lynchseachan
could piece together how it had happened
where his slow, obscure footsteps
led to feathers in the silvered grass.

It may have been him who first spoke
the hawk in the orchard, having seen it;
and then Sweeney, on the trail of his follower,
finally shot past everything into his own
appearance as the panic of the orchard,
such was his hunger to come level
with what he had foreknown.

Once a Man

The hag saw a naked man very briefly
    in the space between a woodcock's design
    and that of a fidgeting siskin.

She saw his bare, skinny arms
    fitting a ruff's headdress,
    his legs disappear into a merganser.

She heard a bunting in a million rushes,
    counting the stems.
When he faltered on the fourth chirp
    she knew it was him.

She remembered how he gargled in the bathroom
    when a raven called.

She could trace where he waited
    to rob a mallard
    in a grove of twayblades

by a mayfly
    writhing in a spiderweb
    and the ivy crucified to the trees —

bitter old hag
    limping back to an outhouse
    with the bulk of a dead goose,

ripping him open, stripping his cover,
    busy in the smoke of his down,

to bring out the man in him
    and hang his goose pimples in her pantry.

Sweeney in Erris

Sweeney sang in a grove of pines
as light skidded off a rippled pool.

A river lost its sweetness seawards.
Oak-leaves gathered on rainy cobbles

where an empire had passed.
Already too late, he sang through the surf

of a windy wood.
Antiquity had been here once. She wrote:

sea trout running every summer,
loaded with stars.

But light and water took them
to be the ghosts of their glen

in the otherworld of a river,
the raven lording.

Now only a linnet was allowed
in a company of thistles.

One rowan couldn't redeem
and was too much to condemn,

rhododendron too deeply rooted
in its own bitter shadow

for anyone to bother. Thistledown
flaked from Sweeney's bill

and swept away to a vastness.

Sweeney Translates

I'm the first flight
under dawn light,
hen of heather,
mason of the egg.

Yellow on red,
siobhán of the fuchsia,
my song carries
in the blowy lane.

When they tried to fix
my wings to a crucifix
they couldn't decide
which quill was my wrist.

So I slipped the bite
of their cold pins
and sing again
within the song of myself.

A Tubenose Skull

As they combed the beaches for Sweeney
they came across an empty shell,

a tubenose skull at the end of earth,
its hooked mandible

remembering the bending sea.
They whispered 'fulmar'

to this rare pelagic flower;
but their lore was no match

for the saga of the ledges,
when a walnut brain

and a fringe of feathers
could contain those calling cliffs.

So the plated beak
became a mask to fit on manners,

a double-barrel breath
steeling the will

to the first drop over an ocean
where Sweeney fell

and then carried on
in the briny stations,

winging it
through every distraction of the weather.

The Burning City

Wader Sweeney
wanted to get to the burning city
but the river was wide at that point   he lost time

crossing over   taking both shores   downwind
he could smell the burning   he flew again
with a flock of undecided dunlins

they switched directions over dark water   he said
'No it's this way'   his words a redshank
scolding the others   he could smell the burning city

the main emotions   on the stiffening wind
pushing the wildfowl back he laboured on
upstream   'What about the kids
in the pleading city?'   his words a curlew

bubbling under the ideal note
when a farmer dropped a crowbar on a stone
the birds detonated in every direction

Sweeney wanted to shout 'It's upstream
to the smouldering city!'   'This way'
said the ringed plover's plaintive note

in all the confusion as the smell changed
and the first soldier kicked over the rubble
of the ruined city

One for Sorrow

At the prime time of May blossom
something grey shoots past at dusk,
hunched under the gloom,
impaired by memory.

Fated to survive,
it lords the lanes and callows,
folded in its robes on a post,
nowhere earning victimhood.

With the big house burnt
and the gamekeeper gone,
no one is left to nail it to its throne
and let it haunt like a god.

Sorrow, to be sure, in the elaborate
care of its preenings.
Without these it would not go far
through the galaxies of flies.

Once, badly shaken by a catapult,
it hove its kite out of parkland
and spent a night
as the eye of river alders.

Ever since, winged on its fear,
it glides down a margin of terror
to the end of a life,
no leisure to ask how one can

live like this, no conscience
to decode its screeching chatter,
whatever it is breaching the peace
of the ruined demesnes.

Resident

He would not obey in early April
and move on with the whoopers.

He stayed
and joined a hunt of swallows
when May failed
and wet roads were strewn with the wreck of sycamores.

His blackbird's song almost drowned
in a brown river frothing at the falls.

As the flood subsided
he was teal wing with a hook
tracking a run of finnock
in a poor year — another poor year!

A crowd had tightened at the crossroads
around a group of morris men,
but he still found a way in
along the feather tips of their hats.

He was in every drifting plume,
like an eiderdown quilt covering lovers.

And when we saw a sparrow on a windy gutter
he put us to the test:

little god of Thor,
blown scruffy-head,
ruffle duster,
eye-liner scallopy,
skip yawn,
chirp-in-gale.

Eorann and the Hag

Eorann: This fabulous headdress. Who made it? Who set him
    on?
Hag: I did. We had nothing to lose one June dawn.

Eorann: And these antlers? They weigh ten pounds at least.
Hag: Oh, he could also play the great beast.

Eorann: None of this stuff fits with the man I knew.
Hag: These were all parts he could master too.

Eorann: Tell me, is this all, or was there more?
Hag: I could see through bird or stag to a man's power.

Eorann: I'm the one who knew it, and I watched it end.
Hag: Whatever happened, you were his greatest friend.

Eorann: Who are you to quote! Was he in your keep?
Hag: Don't let that question trouble your sleep.

Eorann: We'd managed to get him back. He was steady again!
Hag: The creature you captured wasn't the whole man.
When the hunt approached I steeled his fear.
'Don't panic like a bird and leave in a skitter.
Be strong as a stag covering the moor.
Let their horses founder on the swampy floor.'

Eorann: But get to the point! Where is he now?
Hag: I would take you straight to him, if I knew how.

Eorann: It's Sweeney this, Sweeney that — and himself gone!
Hag: You see, he planned his legacy as he moved on.

A Wagtail Gloss

Sweeney danced
        on the peak of a roof,

little alpinist in his crampons
        after a fly,

so high and light!
        Then he settled again,

ahead of his own long wobbling tail —
        only to vanish in a flit,

not caring how the scribe's pen
        had to labour after him

in his economy and freedom.

Notes and Acknowledgements

Tarsaghaunmore (in Irish *Tairseachán Mór*, great threshold; i.e. land on the boundary of another territory) is a townland in the Nephin Beg mountains of North Mayo. The area is a wild, remote expanse of blanket bog with a number of spate rivers draining off the uplands. The townland of Tarsaghaunmore gives its name to one of these rivers.

In its meanders across its flood plain the river has deposited sandy material, allowing a certain amount of better-drained land to form along its banks. It was, presumably, this small advantage which tempted people to settle along the river in the past: several ruined houses at Tarsaghaunmore attest to the forlorn, back-breaking labour of these early settlers.

The modern access road ends close to the river at the adjacent townland of Tarsaghaun Beg, which still boasts three households. Today, the curious visitor has to walk upstream for at least half an hour to reach what is properly the townland of Tarsaghaunmore, now uninhabited and virtually unvisited except by scientists from the Marine Institute checking a rainfall gauge or — rarely — a hiker on the Bangor Trail that crosses the catchment. The atmosphere of abandonment around the house and field remains in this area is unrelieved; even the wildlife of the area offers few distractions, a natural fact compounded by overgrazing.

When I first began to explore here about five years ago I met the late Paddy McHugh who still travelled up and down the river to keep track of his cattle. By then already in his eighties, Paddy was a remnant of a pastoral lifestyle of ancient origin. He was also a voice for the history and folklore of an area whose population has declined to the brink of extinction, and he had memories of the last inhabitant of the even more remote Owenduff catchment travelling home from Bangor with a sack of flour slung across the back of his pony.

Tarsaghaunmore is now within the newly-designated Ballycroy National Park and it therefore has a government guarantee for a future as a scientific reservation. The process of survey and study that accompanies designation as a state wilderness has already started. At the same time this desert makes other claims on our attention: Robert Lloyd Praeger referred to it as 'the very loneliest place in the country' and used it as the occasion for a rare spiritual reflection: 'Go up to the hills, as sages and saints have done since the beginning of the world, and you will need to be a very worldly worldling if you fail to catch some inarticulate vision of the strange equation in which you stand on the one side and the universe on the other.' The word 'inarticulate' certainly seems to go with the terrain; on the other hand, it was against this very feeling of desolation that I wrote the small group of poems in Part One.

Casadh na Leice is the Irish name for a large pool on the river which regularly holds salmon and sea trout.

The river which inspired 'The O———' is a tributary of one of Mayo's best salmon and sea trout rivers. Each year salmon and sea trout return from the sea to spawn in its gravel beds and provide intriguing sport for the rod angler. They have survived despite the pressures of commercial overfishing, pollution, poaching and unscrupulous anglers, and their continuing return to the streams where they were first spawned is part of a pattern that can only be called heroic. These populations of migratory fish, as well as the rivers which sustain them, are one of the oldest elements of Ireland's natural heritage and constitute a treasure beyond price.

During their early years of life in freshwater salmon and sea trout are known as parr. They then undergo physiological change, returning to the sea as smolts. A grilse is a salmon that has returned to its native river after one winter at sea. Redds are the shallow pits excavated in the gravels of river beds by spawning salmon. A spent salmon returning to the sea in early Spring after breeding is termed a kelt.

Canto XIV, *cleamhadh deorán* is a name for the common sandpiper (*tringa hypoleucos*) given to me by Paddy McHugh.

Canto XV, the words in italics are from Robert Lloyd Praeger's *The Way That I Went* (1937).

I wish to acknowledge Caitríona Hastings' help and thank Michael Kingdon, 'the compleat angler', for generous instruction in the craft.

'Bird Sweeney' is based on a familiar story from a medieval Irish poem *Buile Shuibhne*, notably translated by Seamus Heaney as *Sweeney Astray* (1983). In its received form the story of Sweeney's transformation into a bird is clearly told from the prevailing mediaeval Christian viewpoint, a bias which, I imagine, is reflected in the fact that no interest is attached to what kind of bird Sweeney 'actually' became. The idea that Sweeney might have changed successively into different bird species gave me the starting point and allowed me to extend an interest I had explored in a series of bird poems published some years ago as *The Clare Island Survey* (Gallery, 1991).

Finally, I should like to thank the editors of the following publications where some of these poems first appeared: *Irish Pages*, *Poetry Ireland Review*, *Present Tense: Poems and Photographs from County Mayo* (2006), *The SHOp* and *The Yellow Nib*.